HOW TO DRAW
Fairies
AND OTHER PRETTY PICTURES

ARCTURUS

ARCTURUS

This edition published in 2015 by Arcturus Publishing Limited
26/27 Bickels Yard, 151–153 Bermondsey Street,
London SE1 3HA

ISBN: 978-1-78404-486-2
CH004420NT

Written by Lisa Regan
Illustrated by Katy Jackson
Edited by Joe Harris, Samantha Noonan, Samantha Hilton & Frances Evans
This edition produced by JMS Books

Supplier 26, Date 0815, Print run 4546

Printed in China

Contents

Getting started

This book will teach you how to draw a cast of wonderful characters. Simply follow the step-by-step instructions and get drawing!

1. Start with a plain piece of unlined paper. If you are going to paint your picture, you should use thick paper.

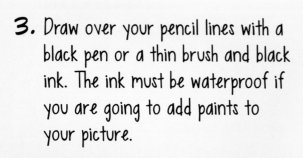

2. Use a pencil to copy the step-by-step instructions. Soft pencils are good for rough sketches. Hard pencils are best for details.

3. Draw over your pencil lines with a black pen or a thin brush and black ink. The ink must be waterproof if you are going to add paints to your picture.

4. When the pen ink has dried, use a large, soft eraser to remove the pencil marks. Now your picture is looking nice and neat!

5. Complete your picture by filling it in with felt-tip pens, pencils, or paint.

6. Paintbrushes come in different shapes. When painting, use a thin, pointed brush for detail and a fatter brush for larger areas.

Fantastic Fairies

Welcome to Fairyland! Meet Marigold, a little flower fairy who loves to soar through the sky and turn somersaults in mid-air.

Queen Rosalind

The beautiful ruler of Fairyland loves to hold parties for all of the woodland fairies in her kingdom.

Fifi the Bug

This little bug lights up the whole of Fairyland with her special glow! She and Marigold always spend their days together.

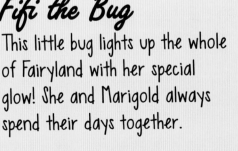

Benjy Butterfly

This adorable butterfly is Queen Rosalind's messenger. He flutters across Fairyland carrying important news!

Sunny the Elf

Weather pixies can choose what the weather will be in Fairyland. They can make it rain, snow, or blow a gale, but guess what Sunny chooses the most?

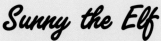

Fairy Willow

Willow is a water sprite who watches over the lakes and pools of Fairyland. She likes to ride in her magical boat and she loves a good water fight!

Fairy Marigold

1. Begin Marigold by drawing an egg shape with a pointed part at the bottom. Sketch a square beneath.

2. Connect the two shapes with her neck. Add the flowery skirt shape below her torso. It starts as a triangle, with points along the bottom edge for petals.

8

3. Draw lines for the shape of her arms and legs. Add circles for her hands and ovals for her feet. Marigold loves to skip and dance!

4. Widen the arms and legs, and draw her fingers and thumbs. Sketch where her flower will be. Now start drawing her face, and don't forget her smile!

5. Sketch in her hair, shoes, and skirt. Then finish her face. She's not quite ready yet!

6. Finish Marigold's outfit with pretty flowers and fairy wings. Fill in her lovely dress and wings with floral shades. Now she's ready to play with her friends!

10

Fairy Willow

1. Begin Willow by drawing an egg shape with a pointed part at the bottom for her head and a small rectangular torso.

2. Connect the two shapes with her neck. Sketch a loose, billowing shape where her skirt will be, and add lines for her arms and legs.

3. Fill out her arms and legs slightly, and add her hands and feet. Reshape her torso a little to give her a willowy waist.

4. Erase the guide lines so that you can see her shape clearly. Sketch the basic features on her face, and add little fingers and toes.

5. Now you can turn her into a true
water sprite! Add lots of wavy hair,
and make the hem of her dress look
like water droplets.

6. Finally, draw in her fantastic wings.
They should look like a water splash!
Add a few lines to give texture to
her hair and clothes. Shade her dress
with beautiful blues and greens.

Sunny the Elf

1. Draw an oval with a pointed bottom part for Sunny's mischievous face. Add a long rectangle for his torso.

2. Add his neck, then sketch in his arms and legs. He looks pretty scrawny at the moment!

3. Now you can give Sunny some clothes. Sketch the outline of his tunic and shorts, then the pointed boots on his feet.

4. Erase the guide lines on his clothes, and fill in his arms and legs. Draw a guide line across his face at a slight angle and sketch his pointed ears and his naughty grin.

5. Fill in the rest of Sunny's face. Now you can have fun adding his spiky hair. He's almost ready to cause some mischief!

6. Finish your wonderful weather elf with a few details on his clothes. Then shade him in using red, orange, and yellow pencils. Add a pair of weather wings. You could copy these lightning bolts or try clouds!

15

Queen Rosalind

1. Rosalind starts off very small! Draw an oval with a slight point at the bottom and a semicircle, just a little way beneath.

2. Add her neck to connect the two shapes. Draw the shape of her flowing gown, then add lines to show where her arm will be.

3. Fill out her arm and add a semicircle for her sleeve. She looks graceful already!

4. Start her face and add in long, flowing hair and pointed ears. Her wings are big because she is the fairy queen.

5. Add a tall, pointed crown, and finish the details on her face. Add shape to the edge of her wings and on her skirt.

6. Decorate and fill in her wings, gown, hair, and crown with regal shades such as purple and gold, fit for a magical queen!

Benjy Butterfly

1. Start Benjy with a round head and long, bean-shaped body. Sketch in small arms and legs.

2. Fill out the arms and legs. Draw two large triangles to make a start on Benjy's brilliant wings.

3. Use the triangles as a guide to make the wings more shapely. Add a happy face with eyes and a mouth.

4. Erase all of your guide lines, so that you can start to add beautiful patterns. Make sure the opposite wings mirror each other.

5. Play around with swirls, loops, and borders. Make Benjy proud to show off his wings!

6. Fill in any gaps with circles and more swirls, then choose some bright shades to decorate his pretty wings. Don't forget to add his antennae, or he won't know where he's going!

Fifi the Bug

1. Draw Fifi's head first. It is a very rounded triangle. Below that, draw an egg shape for her middle.

2. Connect her head and middle with a skinny neck. Sketch part of a circle to form her tail, then add some lines to show where her arms and legs will be.

3. Fill out her arms and legs, then add in her feet and hands. Remember, she might be an insect, but she's very cute!

20

4. Add two ovals for her eyes, a small nose and mouth, and long, twisting antennae.

5. Finish her eyes, then add eyelashes and eyebrows. Draw the shape of her wings behind her.

6. Fill in the detail on her wings, and use bright shades to fill in her body. Then, draw a line across her bottom section, and add lines as light rays to show how she glows in the twilight.

These little fairies have drifted far from home
and have reached a new land!
Draw the magical kingdom they have found.

Midsummer Night Fair

Queen Rosalind has organized a fair for all the fairies. Find the fairies and complete the scene using lots of pretty pencils!

Finish the picture of a beautiful magical castle for the fairies to live in.

26

Pretty Princesses

Princess Polly lives with her sisters in a beautiful faraway kingdom. They love to play with all their magical friends!

Princess Evie

Polly and Natasha's baby sister simply adores being a princess! She loves to try on pretty dresses and tiaras.

Percy Peacock

He's a VIP: a very important peacock! Percy's best friend is Princess Natasha. His magical feathers allow him to talk to humans!

Mother Stardust

Every kingdom should have a fairy godmother! She tries to make everyone's wishes come true.

Princess Natasha

Princess Polly's sister just loves music and dancing. She can't wait for the next grand royal ball!

Moonbeam

This mystical unicorn comes from a distant secret valley. He often uses his magic to help Princess Polly.

Princess Polly

1. Start by drawing an egg shape for her head and a triangle for her body. Nice and simple!

2. Connect the two shapes with her neck, and add some lines to show where her arms go. Sketch a soft triangle below for her beautiful skirt.

3. A line halfway down her face shows where her eyes will be. Give her some pretty flared sleeves and a collar, and then draw in her royal crown!

4. Start drawing her face, and fill out the skirt of her dress a little more. Give it a nice swish!

5. Finish her face with eyelashes and some dainty lips. She needs beautiful long hair flowing down her back.

6. Finally, decorate her dress and her crown, then choose pretty pencils or paints to fill in her dress and hair.

Moonbeam

1. Draw a rectangle and add a semicircle at each end. This will be Moonbeam's body.

2. For his legs, draw two pairs of lines at the front and back. Add another pair to make a bent front leg like you can see here.

3. Moonbeam's head looks a little bit like a pear on its side. Make sure you leave room for his majestic neck!

4. Connect his head and body with two curved lines, then give more shape to his back, stomach, and legs.

5. Draw in his other back leg. Add his eye, mouth, and nostril. Now it's time to give him a beautiful flowing mane and tail.

6. Finish Moonbeam by adding detail to his mane and tail, then drawing his special magical horn. Shade in his body and long hair with an enchanted blue. What magic do you think he will do tonight?

Mother Stardust

1. Draw a rectangle with a pointed lower end for Mother Stardust's head. Sketch in a rectangle for her torso.

2. Add her neck to connect the two shapes, then sketch lines to show where her arms go. She's lifting her wand to cast a spell.

3. Now it's time to draw the shape of her pretty dress. Don't forget the squiggly bit at the bottom!

4. Erase her body guide lines, and draw in her fairy wings. Sketch her face and then the shape of her hair.

5. Finish her face with full lips, eyelashes, and eyebrows. Now add frills to her skirt. It's like a real party dress!

6. Finally, add more detail to her hair, decorate her dress and wings, and draw in a magic wand. Then choose some pretty pencils to shade her in. Now she is ready to grant wishes!

Percy Peacock

1. Percy starts life as a large egg with a small oval hovering just above it.

2. Connect his head and body with curved lines to make a big teardrop shape, then draw a large semicircle. This will be his magnificent tail!

3. Draw a small semicircle inside the first one. Add an eye and a beak. Draw his legs under the body, with little peacock feet.

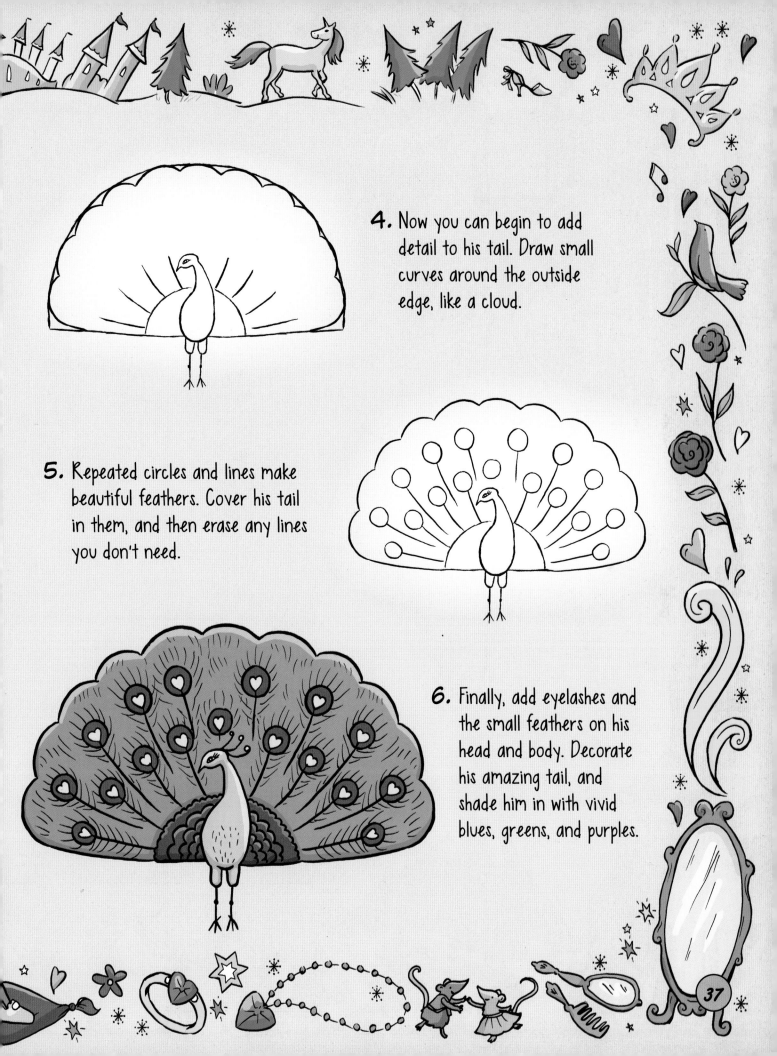

4. Now you can begin to add detail to his tail. Draw small curves around the outside edge, like a cloud.

5. Repeated circles and lines make beautiful feathers. Cover his tail in them, and then erase any lines you don't need.

6. Finally, add eyelashes and the small feathers on his head and body. Decorate his amazing tail, and shade him in with vivid blues, greens, and purples.

Princess Natasha

1. Draw a circle for Princess Natasha's head. Make the bottom end a little bit pointed. Then, draw a larger oval underneath for her torso.

2. Draw her neck and a long triangle for her skirt. Add a fan shape on one side of her torso. Her fluttering fan keeps her cool.

3. Give her arms and hands, then draw the outline for her wavy hair. She's starting to look like a pretty princess!

4. Two eyes, a nose, and a smiley mouth make a lovely start to her face. Next, give more shape to her dress.

5. Finish off her face, then add her beaded headband and the front of her hair.

6. Finally, decorate her fan and give her cool bracelets and earrings. Fill in her regal dress and accessories with deep purples and pinks.

Princess Evie

1. Start Princess Evie by drawing an oval for her head. A square and a curved triangle make the outline of her dress.

2. Draw lines for her arms, with circles to show where her hands will be. Her legs start as two lines with oval feet.

3. Draw circles on her shoulders to make the puffed sleeves of her dress. Then fill out her arms and legs.

4. Add in her eyes, nose, and mouth. Princess Evie is known for her pretty smile!

5. Finish her hands and the cute features on her face. Now sketch in her hair, complete with a neat ponytail.

6. Finally, add detail to her hair and crown her with a tiara. Decorate her dress and shade it in yellow and orange. Put little slippers on her feet, and she is all ready!

The Royal Ball

Fill in this picture of the princesses dancing with their princes in pretty shades. Can you spot the dancing mice and the lost slipper?

43

Mother Stardust is granting another magical wish! Who has made the wish and what are they hoping for?

Moonbeam can use his magic to change his coat to any shade or pattern he likes! Try some new looks for him here.

Purrfect Pets

Barney the pup loves to play with his friends in the Purrfect Pet Shop. He is a happy puppy and is always full of bounces and barks!

Fizzy the Pony

Children come to the Purrfect Pet Shop especially to have a ride on Fizzy's back. He is a gentle and patient pony, and loves the apples that people bring him as a treat.

Cleo the Cat

This cute kitty has the best time playing outside in piles of leaves. She always likes to clean her white paws after, though!

Squeaky the Guinea Pig

She may be small, but Squeaky is a feisty guinea pig. When she wants something, she squeaks and squeaks until she gets it!

Topaz the Goldfish

She's the prettiest fish in the pet shop! Topaz and her sister, Bubbles, live in the same tank, where they play chase around the rocks and ornaments.

Barney the Pup

1. Draw a circle for Barney's head and an oval underneath, but overlapping, for his body.

2. Sketch lines to show where his front legs and paws will go. Add a sausage on each side to start his back legs.

3. Two triangles make his floppy ears, then sketch in the start of his waggly tail! Maybe he is hoping for a treat?

4. Start to draw his cute puppy face. Draw a line at a slight angle and add his eyes. His mouth is two curves. Make his front legs wider.

5. Barney is a panting pup, so draw in his tongue! Then add some fluffy tufts on top of his head.

6. Finally, make him look furry by adding rough lines all around the edges of your drawing. Make his ears rounder and his tail fatter. Choose a sandy pencil to fill in Barney's fur. Woof, woof!

Fizzy the Pony

1. Draw two circles side by side for Fizzy's body. Add his head slightly to the right, like an upside-down teardrop.

2. Connect these shapes with curved lines. Fizzy is coming to life already!

3. Erase the lines you don't need. Draw in his legs with simple lines. The front legs are straight, but the back legs bend backward. Add four hoof shapes.

4. Use your guide lines to help you fill out his legs. They need to be wider at the top.

5. Draw in a thick mane and tail. Don't forget his ears and the forelock in between them. Show Fizzy's cute character with a small eye, mouth, and nostrils.

6. Finally, give Fizzy some shaggy hair around his hooves and a pattern on his coat. Erase any spare lines, and finish his mane and tail. Use different shades of brown for his fur.

Cleo the Cat

1. Cleo starts out as two ovals. The smaller one should be tilted slightly.

2. Sketch little lines to show where her tail and legs will go. Remember, she's a dainty little kitty!

3. Make her face the right shape by drawing in two triangles for ears and a little pointed chin underneath.

4. Add two circles for her eyes, then add a little nose. Make her legs and tail wider, following your lines.

5. Erase any lines you don't need. Add detail to her ears, eyes, and paws. Draw in rough patterns on her fur.

6. Fluff her up with little pencil lines around the edge of her body, and don't forget to draw her whiskers. Use browns and oranges to shade in her fur. Now she's purr-fect!

Squeaky the Guinea Pig

1. Start by drawing a soft, curved triangle for Squeaky's head.

2. Add her body by drawing a large oval. The side of the oval should overlap the head by more than half.

3. Draw two cute little feet at the front and one at the back. She has four feet, of course, but one is hidden in this picture!

4. Sketch in her sweet little face, complete with a snuffling nose. Don't forget her wiggly ears!

5. Erase the top of her head and replace it with some tufty fur on top. Fill in her eye, and add a few little whiskers and dots.

6. Use short pencil strokes to make her fur look more fluffy. Use the same strokes to add a pattern on her back, too. Then use honey shades to create her lovely fur. On your marks, get set, SQUEAK!

Topaz the Goldfish

1. Begin Topaz by drawing a circle. It's as easy as that!

2. Add points at the front and back to shape her body. The back one should be a little more curved than the front.

3. Erase the inner guide lines, and add her fins. She has one large fin on top and two fins underneath.

4. Draw two large tail fins trailing out behind her. Use flowing strokes to get a wonderful, swishing tail.

5. Add her eye and a little mouth. Draw frills at the ends of her fins to make them fancier. She is the prettiest fish in the Purrfect Pet Shop, after all!

6. Add decoration to all her fins, and draw in some scales on her body. Some air bubbles show she is swimming along. Then shade her orange!

The Purrfect Pet Shop
The shop is full of the most adorable creatures. Count all the sleeping animals you can see, then fill in the picture using your best pencils.

Charlie is having a cat nap! Draw what you think he is dreaming about.

Magical Forest

Take a walk in this enchanted forest and meet Greta the squirrel and her friends. These animals are very special... they can talk!

Jack the Bunny

He's such a smart bunny! Not only is he clever, but you'll never see him without his bow tie, and perfectly clean paws.

Amelie the Fawn

This fawn always hears the news first! She trots around the forest, seeing all of her friends and making sure they are having fun.

Bertie the Owl

This clumsy baby owl is always falling out of trees or flying into bushes! Luckily, his soft downy feathers break his fall every time.

Pixie Arya

Years ago, Arya the pixie cast a spell over the forest. All the plants became magical, and the animals began to talk!

Paddy the Cub

Wakey, wakey! Paddy the bear cub just loves to sleep. The magical breeze rocks him in his hammock, high in the trees.

Greta the Squirrel

1. First, draw Greta's head. It is a triangle with rounded corners.

2. Add a teardrop-shaped body. Sketch two little lines to show where her legs and arms will go.

3. Work on the legs and arms to make them fatter and more shapely. She's sitting neatly, ready to go acorn hunting!

4. Erase your guide lines, and then add in her little squirrel face. She's starting to look really cute!

5. Draw her ears and front teeth. Add a large tail, like a backward comma. Fluff out her chest with some extra fur.

6. Make her tail wonderfully big and bushy, and add fluffy pencil lines all around for her fur. Shade her body in light and dark brown or orange, and draw a cute bow on her head. She's off to play with her friends now!

Pixie Arya

1. Start drawing Arya with a circle for her head. Make it pointed at the bottom. Draw a long triangle beneath.

2. Connect the two shapes with her neck, and sketch her arms. Add a long skirt beneath the triangle.

3. Fill out her arms and hands. Draw a line where her waist is, and add feet peeping below her skirt. Arya is always barefoot!

4. Erase the lines you don't need. Draw her eyes and pointed pixie ears, then sketch her nose, mouth, and headband.

5. Add her long, flowing hair and a collar on her dress. Draw in her dainty toes and the detail on her face.

6. Draw a cloak and then have fun decorating her clothes with lots of things from nature. Shade her clothes in greens and browns, like the woodland. Isn't she beautiful?

Jack the Bunny

1. Carefully draw three circles all linked together, like this. He looks a little like a caterpillar at this stage!

2. Join the lower circles to make Jack's body, and add a little nose shape on his face.

3. Sketch the shape of his ears, and draw some cute paws. Now he looks more like a bunny rabbit!

4. Erase the lines you don't need. Draw his face with a big oval eye, and add a fluffy tail on his bottom.

5. Fill in the detail on his eye. It won't be long before he is ready to hop off the page!

6. Finish with his trademark bow tie, and add lots of extra lines to fluff him up around the edges. Shade in his fur so he looks like a real bunny!

Bertie the Owl

1. Bertie starts life as a fat, slightly squashed circle. This will be his head.

2. Draw the same shape, but slightly bigger, underneath. They should overlap each other.

3. Erase the overlapping line, then add two huge eyes. This is so that Bertie can see well in the dark.

4. Draw two frilly circles around the outside of his eyes, then add his beak.

5. Finish his eyes, then add feathery ears and wings. Draw in his little three-toed feet, so he can sit on his branch.

6. Erase the line between his body and head, and draw a small chin. Fill in his body with a combination of shades of brown, then add some downy feathers to make him a real bundle of fluff!

Amelie the Fawn

1. Start by drawing her body. It's the shape of a jelly bean! Add a circle for her head, a little off to the right.

2. Sketch four bent lines to show where her legs will go. She needs them to trot around the forest.

3. Develop her legs so they're the right shape, and add hooves. Connect her head with a curved neck, and draw a pointed snout at the front of her face.

4. Erase all the guide lines so that you can see Amelie's body taking shape. Sketch her perky little tail and two pricked-up ears.

5. Amelie's huge eye is shaped like a leaf. Draw it in, and mark her mouth and nostril.

6. Finish her with the stripe along her head and down her back. Pick some woodland shades for her lovely fur. What a pretty girl she is!

Paddy the Cub

1. Paddy starts out as a large oval with a circle overlapping on the right.

2. Sketch four lines for his little legs, and then add more curve to his cuddly rear end!

3. Fill out his legs so they are stocky and strong. He's ready to take a stroll to find his hammock.

4. Add two round ears and a little fluffy tail. Now you can erase your guide lines. He looks like a real teddy bear!

5. Draw his eyes, nose, and mouth. Add lines to show where the fur on his face changes shade.

6. Have fun making him all furry with rough pencil strokes, and add his paw pads. Shade in all his thick and fluffy fur. Now he's the most cuddly bear in the forest!

Winter Wonderland

Winter has come to the forest and brought a fluffy covering of snow. How many of the animals are wearing a warm scarf?

83

It's about time Paddy stopped snoozing.
Draw someone or something to wake him up.

84

Arya's beautiful dress changes with the seasons. Design a winter dress and a summer dress for her.

Fashion Friends

Grace and her friends love fashion and run their own Belle Boutique. It is full of wonderful clothes they have designed and made themselves. Grace is a great seamstress!

Belle the Dog

Their four-legged friend is so important to the girls that they named their boutique after her. You will never see Belle without her bow!

Chic Stephanie

This girl is SO good at sewing and embroidery! She adds gorgeous details to the outfits that Grace makes.

Fab Phoebe

Hair is Phoebe's thing! She often experiments on her own, and her customers come from miles around to try her new styles.

Sassy Sophie

Super trendy Sophie loves to help everyone look fabulous! All the customers take her advice on what's stylish and cool.

Glamorous Grace

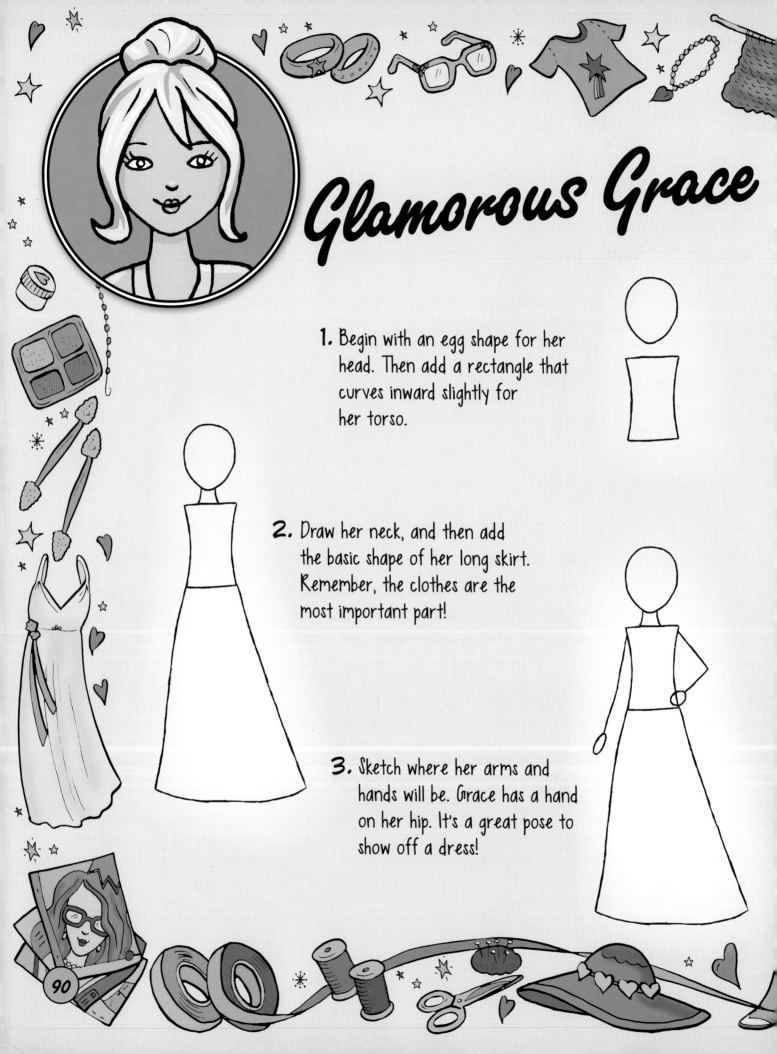

1. Begin with an egg shape for her head. Then add a rectangle that curves inward slightly for her torso.

2. Draw her neck, and then add the basic shape of her long skirt. Remember, the clothes are the most important part!

3. Sketch where her arms and hands will be. Grace has a hand on her hip. It's a great pose to show off a dress!

4. Draw her eyes, nose, and mouth. Fill in her arms, and draw fingers on her hands.

5. Erase your guide lines. Finish her features, and draw the hair that frames her face.

6. Now you can concentrate on the gorgeous design of her dress. Add ruffles to the skirt and detail around the neckline. Choose some pretty pencils to decorate it any way you like!

Sassy Sophie

1. Draw Sophie's head and torso first. The head is slightly pointed at the bottom, and the torso curves inward at the middle.

2. Draw the neck in between, and add a short skirt. The skirt should flare out a little. That's how Sophie likes it.

3. Sketch bent lines for her arms and legs. Add ovals for her hands and feet. She's in a walking pose.

4. Fill out Sophie's arms and legs, and add her face. Give her a pair of cute little boots.

5. Erase the guide lines. Time to add a stylish hairdo and detail to her face and clothes.

6. Now you can have great fun with her outfit! Use cool shades for her clothes, and go to town with patterns, textures, and accessories to make Sophie the most stylish girl around!

Fab Phoebe

1. Start by drawing Phoebe's head and torso. Her head should have a slightly pointed chin, and her torso curves in at the sides.

2. Draw in her neck, and add the shape of her skirt. Sketch in her arms and legs, and add ovals for her feet and hands.

3. Fill out her arms and legs. Add fingers to her hands and shoes on her feet. Phoebe wears cool high-top sneakers!

4. Erase any lines you don't need. Draw her eyes, mouth, and nose. She's starting to take shape.

5. Sketch where her hair will be, and add a belt, neckline, and sleeves to her dress.

6. Finally, decorate her clothes with stars and shade them as you like. Go wild with her hair, since that's what makes Phoebe stand out from the crowd!

Chic Stephanie

1. Start with a pointed oval and a curved rectangle.

2. Draw Stephanie's neck and skirt with a frilled bottom edge. She loves pretty outfits.

3. Draw lines to show where you want her legs and arms to go. She's standing in a neat, dainty pose.

4. Fill out her arms and legs. Add her eyes, a small nose, and mouth. Stephanie is always smiling!

5. Finish her eyes and lips. Erase the guide lines, so that you can draw in the shape of her top and shoes. Sketch the outline of her hair.

6. Now for the part that Stephanie does best, decorations! Choose bright tones for her clothes. Don't forget to add patterns, jewels, and pretty embroidery. The more, the better!

Belle the Dog

1. Draw a shape like a fat number eight. This will be Belle's face and the front part of her body.

2. Give her two little triangular ears. Draw her eyes and nose and a wide, curved mouth. She's such a happy dog!

3. Draw her eyebrows and a tongue sticking out of her mouth. Add a circle for the back of her body.

4. Use lines to show where her curved tail will be and also her four legs. Her back legs are bent. Add four circles for her paws.

5. Give her a big, fluffy tail with lots of pencil strokes following the guide line. Make her legs wider.

6. Now fluff out her body and face, so that she's a big bundle of fur. Then begin to fill in her fur with pretty shades. Draw her a special bow, and she's all ready to greet the customers!

Sophie wants to put together a mood board for a pretty, romantic outfit. Can you doodle your ideas?

Grace is working on a fun, new party collection.
Draw the outfits she has made!

Belle Boutique

The girls are having a busy day at the boutique. Can you spot the cardigan with the flowers on?

104

Under the Sea

Sylvie the mermaid lives in a magic lagoon on a secret tropical island. She spends her time there laughing and splashing with all of her friends.

Twinkle Star

This giggling little starfish loves telling jokes! She is always listening out for funny stories to tell her friends.

Sammy the Seal

He's a bit slow on land, but he's one of the speediest swimmers in the lagoon! He can often be found sunbathing on the rocks to dry his fluffy coat.

Coral the Seahorse

She's beautiful and she knows it! Coral the seahorse spends hours admiring her reflection in shiny shells and gets very upset if anyone ruffles her fins!

Dylan the Dolphin

He isn't any old dolphin, Dylan is a magical dolphin who can cast spells with a swish of his starry tail!

Pearl

She is Sylvie's best friend, and a champion diver. She enters all the mermaid diving contests, and usually wins first prize!

Mermaid Sylvie

1. Sylvie has a long oval for a face, with a pointed end for her chin. Draw a triangle for her body, and connect the two with a slender neck.

2. Sketch a long, thin comma shape for her tail. Add two large, frilled fins at the end. Draw lines where you want her arms to be.

3. Make her arms thicker, and add shape to the ovals of her hands. Draw eyes, a tiny nose, and a mouth. She looks so serene!

4. Begin her hair with two wispy lines, and finish the features on her face. Draw the outline of her top, and then erase any guide lines.

5. Add lots and lots of hair around her face and flowing down her back. Then sketch in the rock and waves of the lagoon.

6. Add lots of pretty details, such as patterns and accessories. Sylvie loves to wear shells! Finish the picture by filling her in with magical pink and purple tones.

Mermaid Pearl

1. Draw an oval face, tilted slightly to one side. Add a sleek curve to show where Pearl's torso and tail will be.

2. Following the curve, draw in a triangular torso and a teardrop-shaped tail. Add two large tail fins on the very end.

3. Erase the guide lines, then draw in her neck, face, and arms. She is swimming sideways!

4. Finish the details on her face, and sketch the shape of her hair on her forehead. Make her arms fuller, and add fingers on each hand.

5. Have fun drawing in her beautiful, wavy hair. Draw the shape of her top and the frill around her waist.

6. Erase any lines you don't need. Add lots of decorations on her clothes, hair, and tail. Don't forget the pearls she is named after! Then shade her outfit in lovely nautical blues.

Coral the Seahorse

1. Draw a semicircle on its side to start Coral's body. This will be her cute little rounded tummy!

2. Add two curves, top and bottom, for Coral's neck and tail. Try to make them as smooth as you can.

3. Extend the tail curve into a spiral. Whee! Draw a circle by the top curve for the head, with a little pointed snout in front.

4. Fill in the gap between her head and body with a graceful neck. Add a smile and an eye. Make the tail into a full spiral.

5. Erase all of the guide lines. Draw the frilly fins on her back, and she is almost ready!

6. Decorate her body and along her back. Add detail to her fins, and draw the streamers on top of her head. Then use pretty pastel shades for her body. Gorgeous!

Twinkle Star

1. Start your star shape with a central dot and three lines going from it. Nice and simple!

2. Draw two more lines going up. They look a lot like arms, even though Twinkle doesn't really have any!

3. Now draw the outside lines, following the direction of the guide lines. Imagine that you are drawing a pointed flower.

4. Erase an area in the middle, so that you can draw two eyes and a little smiling mouth.

5. Finish her mouth so that Twinkle is smiling. She has probably just thought of another joke. Draw tiny circles along the lines on each leg.

6. Keep adding smaller circles and then dots to finish the pattern on Twinkle's body. Choose a shade you like to help Twinkle stand out. Add the small movement lines to show that she is giggling!

Dylan the Dolphin

1. Dylan begins as a slanted oval, nice and simple.

2. Add two curved lines, meeting at a point, for his magical tail.

3. Add a curved triangle on his back for his fin. Draw lines to show where his flippers and tail fins will go.

4. Finish the actual shapes of his flippers and his tail fins. He's starting to take on his super, streamlined form!

5. Draw an eye and a beak-shaped nose. Don't forget, dolphins are always smiling!

6. Erase the few leftover guide lines, and add some splashes of water. Decorate his lower body with magical, sparkling stars and use blues, pinks, and purples to shade him in.

Sammy the Seal

1. Draw a circle, then add two semicircles on the lower edge to make Sammy's chubby little cheeks.

2. Add a leaf shape for his body. The end almost completely overlaps his head. This shape helps him to be a great swimmer.

3. Erase the lines you don't need. Draw in curved lines to show Sammy's flippers and tail.

4. Draw two large circular eyes, halfway down his face. Add a curve over his nose and two curves for his mouth. Make his flippers the right shape.

5. Finish his eyes, and add a V-shaped nose and cute little eyebrows.

6. Complete Sammy with some whiskers, and add some rough lines to make his body furry. Use a light brown for his fur, or leave him pure white. He's all ready to swim away!

Pearl is going to visit the magical underwater mermaid city.
What do you think it looks like?

Diving for Pearls

Look what a beauty Sylvie and Pearl have found! Can you spot four sparkling rings on the sandy floor of the lagoon?

The fish in the magical lagoon are all so beautiful! Shade them in and then draw a new magical friend. What special powers does he or she have?